There are hundreds
and hundreds of reasons
why this book had to
be written - turn
to the back to see
just a few . . .

Fractions

To find a fraction a shape must be divided into equal parts

$$\frac{3}{4}$$

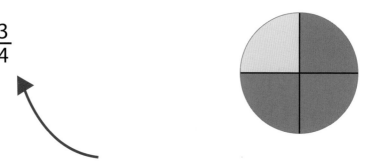

Bottom number = denominator
(all the bits in the fraction)

Top number = numerator
(tells you how many out of the bottom number)

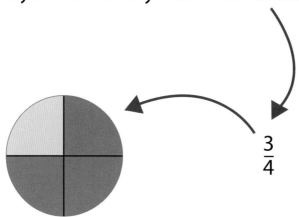

$$\frac{3}{4}$$

Equivalent Fractions

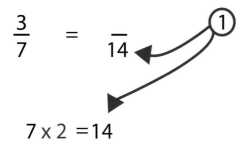

$$\frac{3}{7} = \frac{}{14}$$

① Find out what they have done

$7 \times 2 = 14$

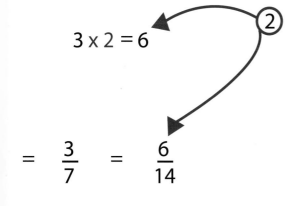

② Do the same

$3 \times 2 = 6$

$$= \frac{3}{7} = \frac{6}{14}$$

Simplifying or Cancelling Fractions

$\dfrac{5}{15}$ ①   ÷ top and bottom by the same number

②   Stop when you can only divide by one

$= \dfrac{1}{3}$

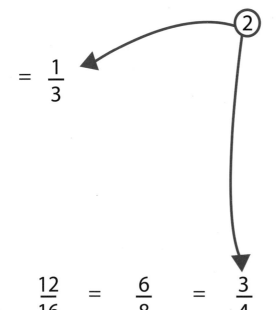

$$\dfrac{12}{16} \;=\; \dfrac{6}{8} \;=\; \dfrac{3}{4}$$

To find a Fraction of a Number

$\frac{2}{5}$ of 35 =

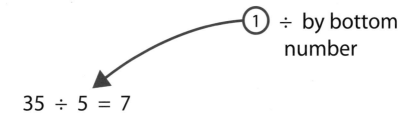

(1) ÷ by bottom number

35 ÷ 5 = 7

(2) x by top number

7 x 2 = 14

$\frac{2}{5}$ of 35 = 14

Improper Fractions to Mixed Number.

Improper fractions = top heavy fractions

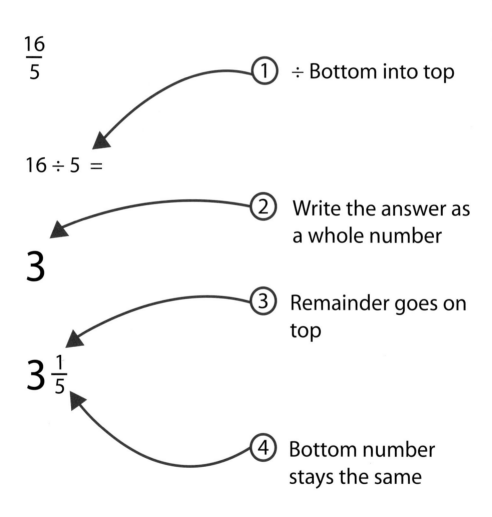

$\dfrac{16}{5}$

① ÷ Bottom into top

$16 \div 5 =$

② Write the answer as a whole number

3

③ Remainder goes on top

$3\dfrac{1}{5}$

④ Bottom number stays the same

Mixed Numbers to Improper Fractions

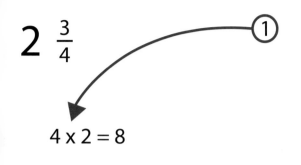

$2 \frac{3}{4}$

① x bottom number and whole number

$4 \times 2 = 8$

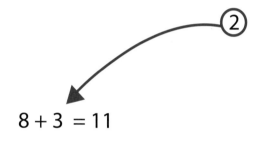

② + top number

$8 + 3 = 11$

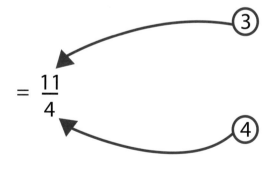

③ Write on top

$= \frac{11}{4}$

④ Bottom number stays the same

Fractions to Percentages

(Percentage = out of 100)

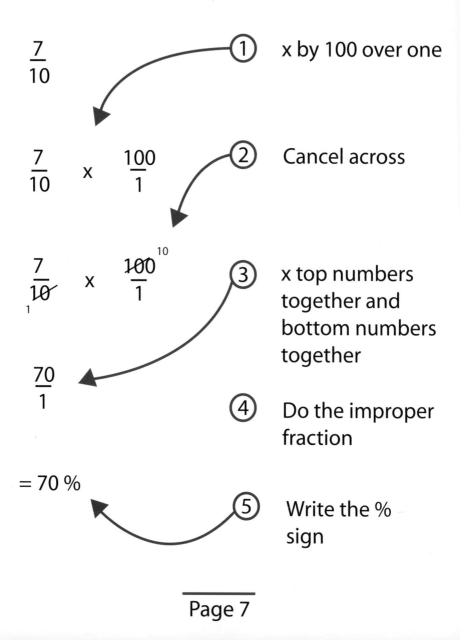

$\dfrac{7}{10}$ ① x by 100 over one

$\dfrac{7}{10}$ × $\dfrac{100}{1}$ ② Cancel across

$\dfrac{7}{\cancel{10}_{1}}$ × $\dfrac{\cancel{100}^{10}}{1}$ ③ x top numbers together and bottom numbers together

$\dfrac{70}{1}$ ④ Do the improper fraction

$= 70\,\%$ ⑤ Write the % sign

Fractions Addition & Subtraction

If the bottom numbers are the same
just add or subtract the top numbers

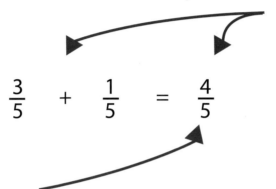

$$\frac{3}{5} \ + \ \frac{1}{5} \ = \ \frac{4}{5}$$

The bottom number stays the same

If the bottom numbers are the same
just add or subtract the top numbers

$$\frac{2}{3} \ - \ \frac{1}{3} \ = \ \frac{1}{3}$$

The bottom number stays the same

Fractions Addition

If the bottom numbers are different

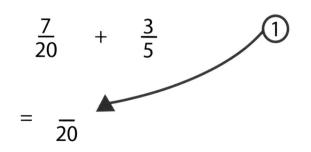

$$\frac{7}{20} \quad + \quad \frac{3}{5}$$

$$= \quad \frac{}{20}$$

① Make the bottom number the same (a number they both divide into)

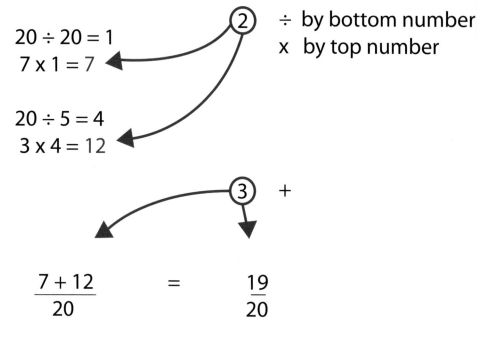

$20 \div 20 = 1$
$7 \times 1 = 7$

$20 \div 5 = 4$
$3 \times 4 = 12$

② ÷ by bottom number
x by top number

③ +

$$\frac{7 + 12}{20} \qquad = \qquad \frac{19}{20}$$

Fractions   Subtraction

the bottom numbers are different

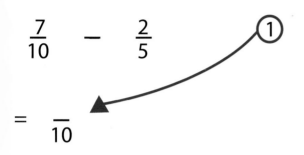

$$\frac{7}{10} \quad - \quad \frac{2}{5}$$

① Make the bottom
number the same
(a number they
both divide into)

$$= \quad \frac{}{10}$$

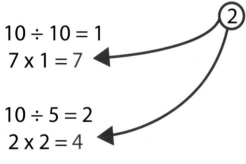

$10 \div 10 = 1$

$7 \times 1 = 7$

② ÷ by bottom number
x by top number

$10 \div 5 = 2$

$2 \times 2 = 4$

③ —

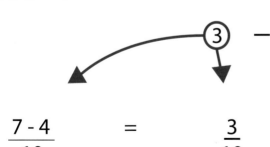

$$\frac{7 - 4}{10} \qquad = \qquad \frac{3}{10}$$

Fractions   Multiplication

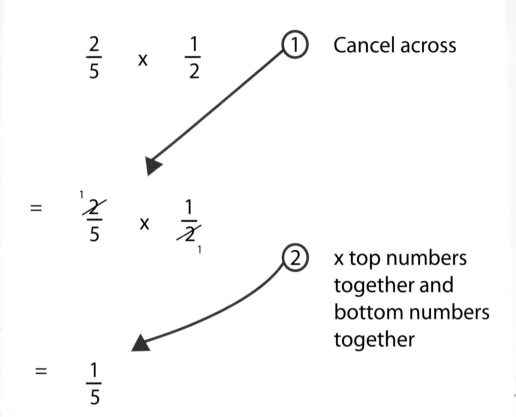

$$\frac{2}{5} \quad \times \quad \frac{1}{2}$$

① Cancel across

$$= \quad \frac{\overset{1}{\cancel{2}}}{5} \quad \times \quad \frac{1}{\underset{1}{\cancel{2}}}$$

② x top numbers together and bottom numbers together

$$= \quad \frac{1}{5}$$

Fractions Division

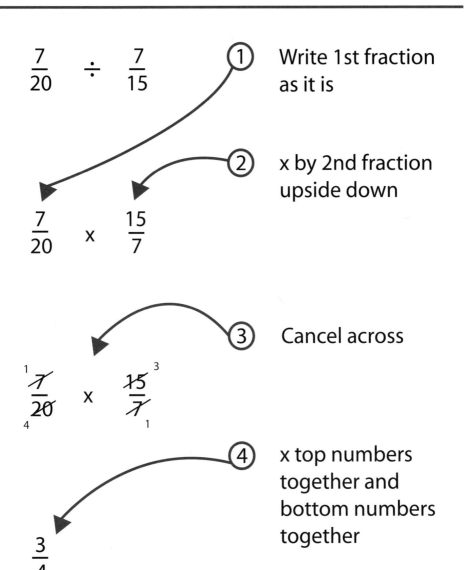

$$\frac{7}{20} \div \frac{7}{15}$$

(1) Write 1st fraction as it is

$$\frac{7}{20} \times \frac{15}{7}$$

(2) x by 2nd fraction upside down

$$= \quad \frac{{}^{1}\cancel{7}}{\cancel{20}_{4}} \times \frac{\cancel{15}^{\,3}}{\cancel{7}_{1}}$$

(3) Cancel across

$$= \quad \frac{3}{4}$$

(4) x top numbers together and bottom numbers together

Place Value

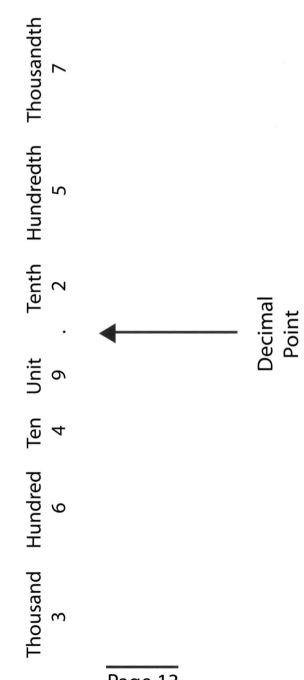

Thousand	Hundred	Ten	Unit	.	Tenth	Hundredth	Thousandth
3	6	4	9	.	2	5	7

← Decimal Point

Place Value

3 6 4 9 . 2 5 7 = 3000

3 6 4 9 . 2 5 7 = 600

3 6 4 9 . 2 5 7 = 40

3 6 4 9 . 2 5 7 = 9 units

3 6 4 9 . 2 5 7 = 2 tenths

3 6 4 9 . 2 5 7 = 5 hundredths

3 6 4 9 . 2 5 7 = 7 thousandths

Consecutive Numbers

Follow each other, one after another

4, 5, 6

An easy way to add three consecutive numbers is to multiply the middle number by 3

$6 + 7 + 8 = 21$ $(3 \times 7 = 21)$

How to find the number halfway between 15 and 27

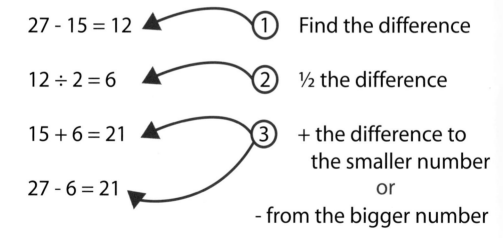

$27 - 15 = 12$	①	Find the difference
$12 \div 2 = 6$	②	½ the difference
$15 + 6 = 21$	③	+ the difference to the smaller number
$27 - 6 = 21$		or
		- from the bigger number

The number halfway between 15 and 27 is 21

Missing Numbers

You double a number and add 3.
The result is 23.
What is the number?

$\square$ x 2 + 3 = 23

① Do it backwards

② Do the opposite

$(+,-)\ (x,\div)$

$\square$ x 2 + 3 = 23
23 − 3 ÷ 2 = $\boxed{10}$

Missing number = 10

Square Numbers

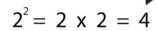

$$2^2 = 2 \times 2 = 4$$

$$3^2 = 3 \times 3 = 9$$

$$4^2 = 4 \times 4 = 16$$

$$5^2 = 5 \times 5 = 25$$

Square root

Square root of $36 = 6$

$(6 \times 6 = 36)$

Square root can also be written

$$\sqrt{36} = 6$$

Cube Numbers

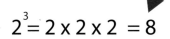

$2^3 = 2 \times 2 \times 2 = 8$

$3^3 = 3 \times 3 \times 3 = 27$

$4^3 = 4 \times 4 \times 4 = 64$

Cube root

Cube root of $125 = 5$

$(\ 5 \times 5 \times 5 = 125\ )$

Factors

Numbers which divide into a number

Factors of $20 = 1 , 20 , 2 , 10 , 4 , 5$

because they all divide into 20

Factors of $20 = 1 , 2 , 4 , 5 , 10 , 20$

A Prime Factor = a factor which is also a prime number.

The prime factors of 20
    $= 2$ and 5

20 can be expressed as a product of its prime factors
    $= 2 \times 5 \times 2$

Prime Numbers

A prime number has two factors and can only be divided by itself and one

2   ,   3   ,   5
(2 x 1)   (3 x 1)   (5 x 1)

7   ,   11   etc
(7 x 1)   (11 x 1)

2 is the first prime number and the only even prime number

1 is not a prime number because it only has one factor

Rounding Numbers

To the nearest 10

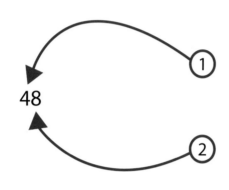

① Find the ten

② Look at the number to its right

③ If it is 5 or more, add one to the ten

Or

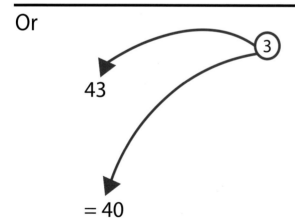

③ If the number on the right is lower than 5, the ten stays the same

Rounding Numbers

o the nearest 100

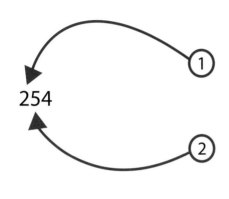

(1) Find the hundred

(2) Look at the number to its right

(3) If it is 5 or more, add one to the hundred

Or

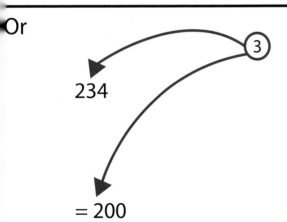

(3) If the number on the right is lower than 5, the hundred stays the same

Re-write correct to one decimal place

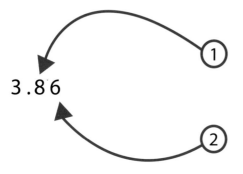

3 . 8 6

(1) Find 1st decimal place

(2) Look at the number to its right

= 3 . 9

(3) If it is 5 or more, add one to 1st decimal place

Or

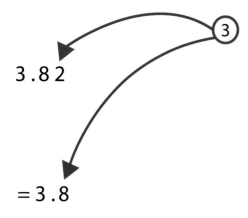

3 . 8 2

(3) If the number on the right is lower than 5, the 1st decimal place stays the same

= 3 . 8

Re-write correct to 2 decimal places

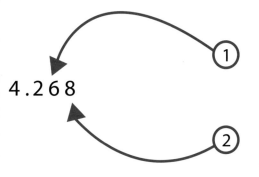

4 . 2 6 8

① Find 2nd decimal place

② Look at the number to its right

= 4 . 2 7

③ If it is 5 or more, add one to 2nd decimal place

Or

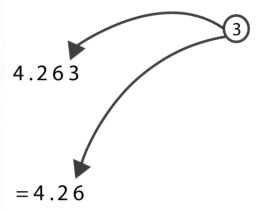

4 . 2 6 3

③ If the number on the right is lower than 5, the 2nd decimal place stays the same

= 4 . 2 6

Perimeter   Area   Volume

Perimeter
(Think of it as
a fence)

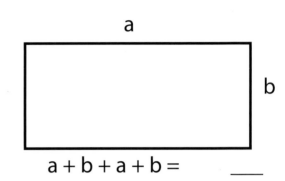

a

b

$$a + b + a + b = \underline{\quad}$$

Area
(Think of it as
a carpet)

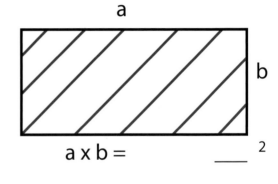

a

b

$$a \times b = \underline{\quad}^2$$

Volume
(Think of it as
air in a room)

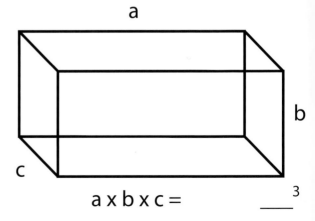

a

b

c

$$a \times b \times c = \underline{\quad}^3$$

Area of an Irregular Shape

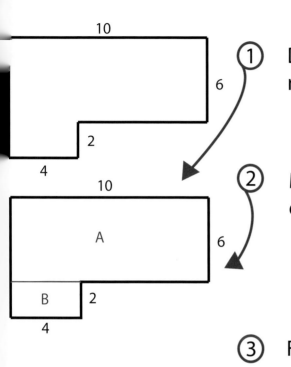

① Divide it into 2 regular shapes

② Mark one A and the other B

③ Find the area of A

Area of A = 10 x 6 = 60cm^2

④ Find the area of B

Area of B = 4 x 2 = 8cm^2

⑤ + the answers

$$\begin{array}{l} 60 \text{ cm}^2 \\ +\ \ 8 \text{ cm}^2 \\ \hline 68 \text{ cm}^2 \end{array} = \text{Total area}$$

Area

Area of a rectangle = base x height

Area of a triangle = 1/2 base x perpendicular height

Area of a parallelogram = base x perpendicular heigh

Area of a circle = πr^2 (r = radius)

$3.14159 = \pi$

Lines

Horizontal = —————— Vertical =

Perpendicular =

Parallel =

Intersection =
(the point where
two lines meet)

Angles

All angles on
a straight
line = 180°

All angles in
a triangle
= 180°

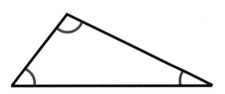

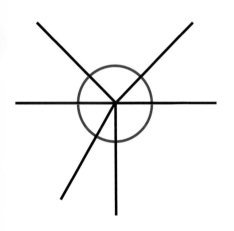

All angles
round a point
or in a circle
= 360°

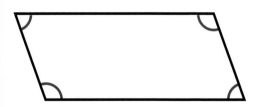

All angles in
a quadrilateral
= 360°

Angles

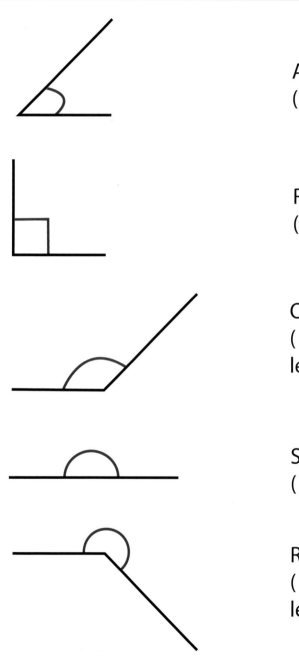

Acute angle
(less than 90°)

Right angle
(90°)

Obtuse angle
(more than 90°
less than 180°)

Straight angle
(180°)

Reflex angle
(more than 180°
less than 360°)

Triangles

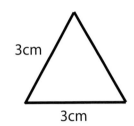

3cm

3cm

Equilateral triangle
(all sides equal
all angles 60°)

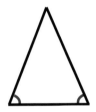

Isosceles triangle
(2 sides equal
2 angles equal)

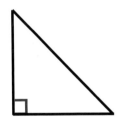

Right - angled
triangle
(one angle = 90°)

Scalene triangle
(no sides equal
no angles equal)

Shapes

Rhombus
(Squashed square)
all sides equal

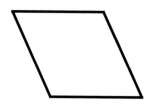

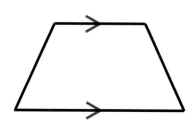

Trapezium
(One set of parallel
sides)

Parallelogram
(Squashed rectangle)
two sets of parallel
sides

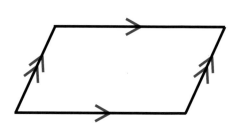

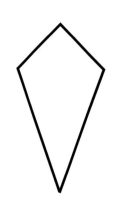

Kite
(two sets of equal
but not parallel sides)

Polygons

Polygon = many sided figure

Regular polygon = equal sided figure

Triangle = 3 sides

Quadrilateral = 4 sides

Pentagon = 5 sides

Hexagon = 6 sides

Heptagon = 7 sides

Octagon = 8 sides

Nonagon = 9 sides

Decagon = 10 sides

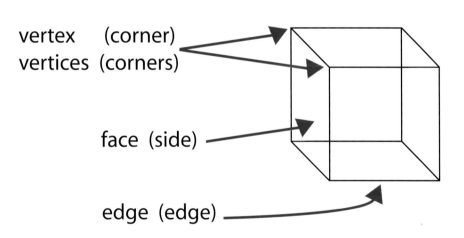

vertex   (corner)
vertices (corners)

face (side)

edge (edge)

A cube has 8 vertices 6 faces 12 edges

Coordinates

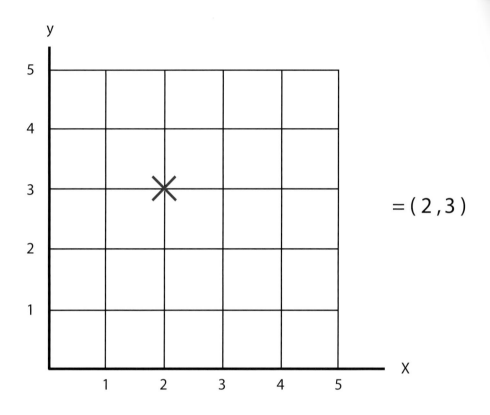

$= (2 , 3)$

The X coordinate (along) is written first,
then the Y coordinate (up)

`Along the corridor and up the stairs´
is a helpful way to remember

Line Graph

To show the number of fine days in a year

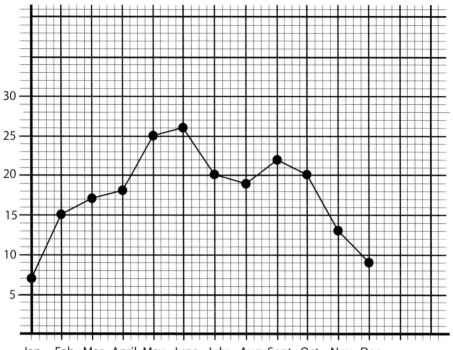

January had 7 days
February had 15 days
March had 17 days
April had 18 days
May had 25 days
June had 26 days
July had 20 days
August had 19 days
September had 22 days
October had 20 days
November had 13 days
December had 9 days

Bar Chart

A bar chart to show Favourite colours

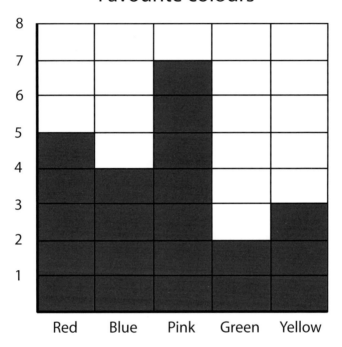

5 people liked red best
4 people liked blue best
7 people liked pink best
2 people liked green best
3 people liked yellow best

Pie Chart

A pie chart to show the favourite
sports of 32 children

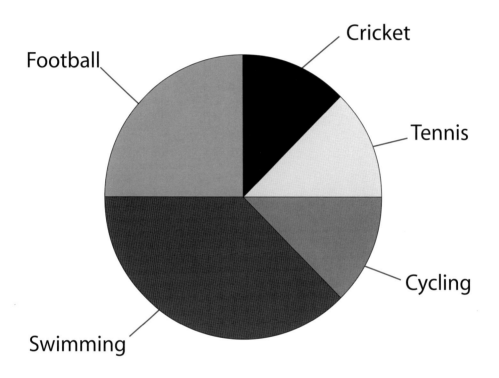

8 people liked football best
4 people liked cricket best
4 people liked tennis best
4 people liked cycling best
12 people liked swimming best

Venn Diagram

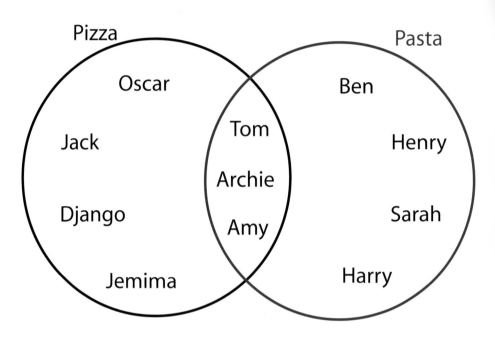

Pizza

Pasta

Oscar

Ben

Jack

Tom

Henry

Archie

Django

Sarah

Amy

Jemima

Harry

both pizza and pasta

Oscar, Jack, Django and Jemima like pizza only

Ben, Henry, Sarah and Harry like pasta only

Tom, Archie and Amy like both pizza and pasta.

Pictogram

Walk	𝅘 𝅘 𝅘 𝅘
Car	𝅘 𝅘 𝅘 𝅘 𝅘 𝅘 𝅘 𝅘
Bus	𝅘 𝅘 𝅘 𝅘 𝅘 𝅘
Cycle	𝅘 𝅘

𝅘 = 2 children

8 children walk to school
16 children go to school by car
12 children travel by bus
4 children cycle to school

Circumference, Diameter, Radius

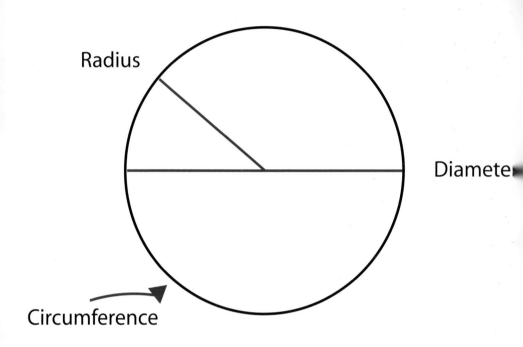

Circumference = all round the edge

Diameter = distance across the middle

Radius = distance from the edge to the middle
(1/2 diameter)

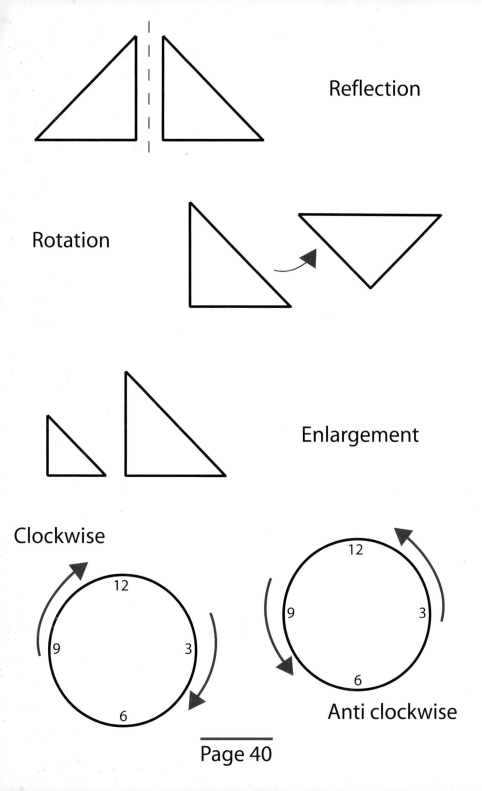

Reflection

Rotation

Enlargement

Clockwise

Anti clockwise

Symmetry

A line which makes one half of a shape look exactly like the other half

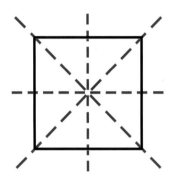

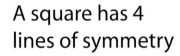

A square has 4 lines of symmetry

A kite has 1 line of symmetry

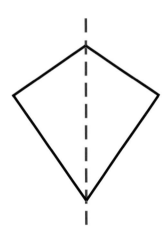

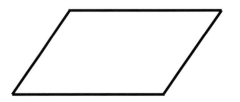

A parallelogram has no lines of symmetry

Rotational Symmetry

A shape that can be turned to fit exactly on to itself has Rotational Symmetry

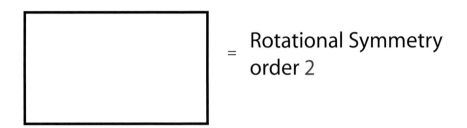 = Rotational Symmetry order 2

It can be turned to fit back on to itself in 2 different ways

Rotation Symmetry order 4 =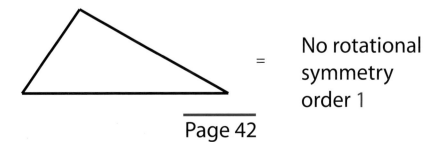

It can be turned to fit back on to itself in 4 different ways

No rotational symmetry order 1

Ratio

Ratio is a way of comparing different quantities

Tom is 7 years old and Polly is 11 years old.
What is the ratio of Tom's age to Polly's?

$$7 : 11$$

Ratio is usually written with a colon

Always cancel ratios to their lowest terms

Write the ratio 6 : 8 : 12 in its lowest terms.

They can all be divided by 2.

so 3 : 4 : 6 is the correct ratio

Ratio

Sam and Sally share £35.00
in the ratio of 2 : 3
How much money do they each have?

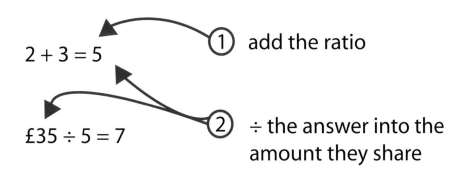

$2 + 3 = 5$ ① add the ratio

$£35 \div 5 = 7$ ② ÷ the answer into the
amount they share

Sam has 2 lots of £7
Sally has 3 lots of £7

Sam = 2 x 7 = £14.00

Sally = 3 x 7 = £21.00

Probability

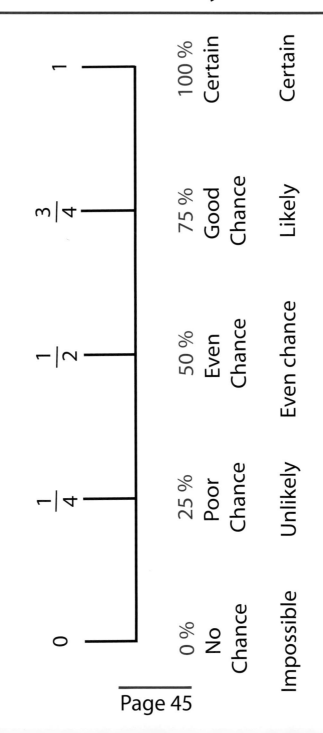

	0	$\frac{1}{4}$	$\frac{1}{2}$	$\frac{3}{4}$	1
	0 %	25 %	50 %	75 %	100 %
	No Chance	Poor Chance	Even Chance	Good Chance	Certain
	Impossible	Unlikely	Even chance	Likely	Certain

Probability

There are 6 balls in a bag.
One pink, 2 blue and 3 red.
What is the probability of picking a red one?

alls = 6   ①   Add up all
the balls

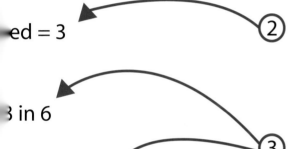

ed = 3   ②   Find out how
many red ones
there are

3 in 6

    ③   Cancel

= 1 in 2 chance = $\frac{1}{2}$

You have a : -

$\frac{1}{6}$ or 1 : 6 chance of throwing 6 with a dice

$\frac{1}{2}$ or 1 : 2 chance of getting heads on a coin

Averages

Mode = The number which occurs most often

3 , 5 , 3 , 7 , 9 , 3 , 4

Mode = 3

Median = The middle number after they have been placed in order

9 , 2 , 6 , 3 , 5

= 2 , 3 , (5) , 6 , 9

Median = 5

Averages

Mean Average

7 , 32 , 34

93

3 ÷ 3 = 31

mean / average = 31

① add all the numbers

② Divide by how many numbers you added

Range = The difference between the largest and smallest numbers

37 , 21 , 19 , 25

(37 - 19)

range = 18

Percentage = Fraction = Decimal

$$100\% = \text{all of it} = \frac{10}{10} = 1$$

$$75\% = \frac{3}{4} = 0.75$$

$$50\% = \frac{1}{2} = 0.5$$

$$25\% = \frac{1}{4} = 0.25$$

$$10\% = \frac{1}{10} = 0.1$$

$$1\% = \frac{1}{100} = 0.01$$

Percentages to Fractions

15 %

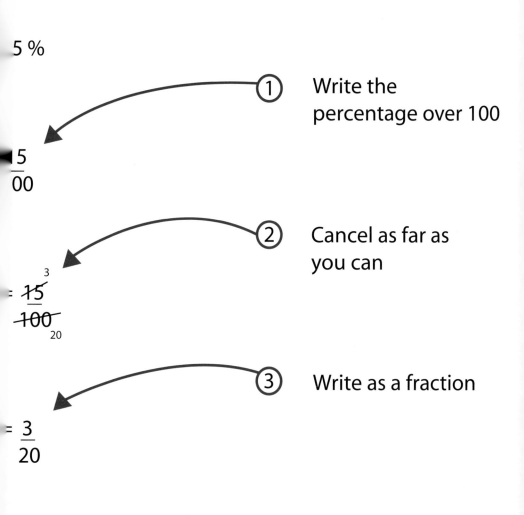

$$\frac{15}{100}$$

① Write the percentage over 100

$$= \frac{\overset{3}{\cancel{15}}}{\underset{20}{\cancel{100}}}$$

② Cancel as far as you can

$$= \frac{3}{20}$$

③ Write as a fraction

Percentages to Decimals

18 %

18 ÷ 100

① ÷ by 100

= 0 . 18

② Write as a decimal

Decimals to Percentages

0.7

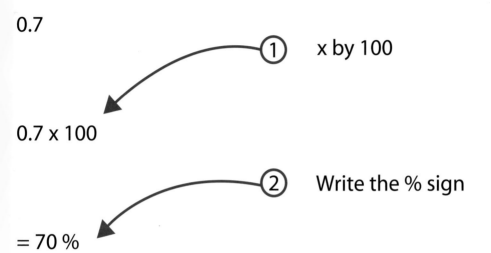

0.7 x 100

① x by 100

② Write the % sign

= 70 %

A Number as a Percentage of a Numbe[r]

What is 17 as a percentage of 20?

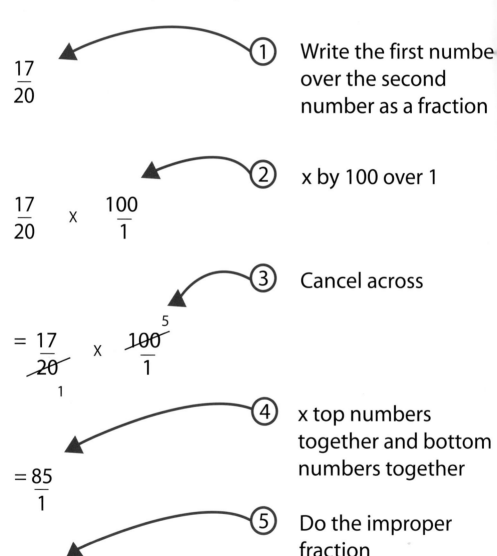

$\dfrac{17}{20}$

(1) Write the first numbe[r] over the second number as a fraction

$\dfrac{17}{20}$ X $\dfrac{100}{1}$

(2) x by 100 over 1

(3) Cancel across

$= \dfrac{17}{\cancel{20}_{\,1}}$ X $\dfrac{\cancel{100}^{\,5}}{1}$

(4) x top numbers together and bottom numbers together

$= \dfrac{85}{1}$

(5) Do the improper fraction

$= 85\%$

To Find a Percentage of a Number

30 % of £400 =

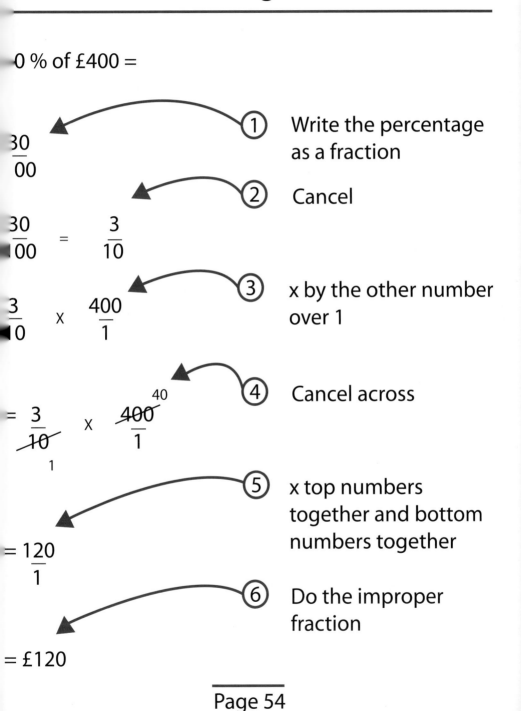

$$\frac{30}{100}$$

① Write the percentage as a fraction

$$\frac{30}{100} = \frac{3}{10}$$

② Cancel

$$\frac{3}{10} \quad \times \quad \frac{400}{1}$$

③ x by the other number over 1

$$= \frac{3}{\cancel{10}_1} \quad \times \quad \frac{\cancel{400}^{40}}{1}$$

④ Cancel across

⑤ x top numbers together and bottom numbers together

$$= \frac{120}{1}$$

⑥ Do the improper fraction

$$= £120$$

Long Multiplication (Method 1)

$34 \times 25 =$

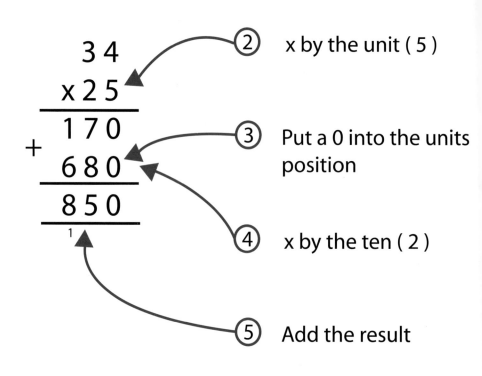

$$\begin{array}{r} 34 \\ \times 25 \\ \hline 170 \\ + \quad 680 \\ \hline 850 \\ \hline \end{array}$$

①   Set it out with tens and units in columns

②   x by the unit (5)

③   Put a 0 into the units position

④   x by the ten (2)

⑤   Add the result

$34 \times 25 = 850$

Long Multiplication (Method 2)

34 x 25 =

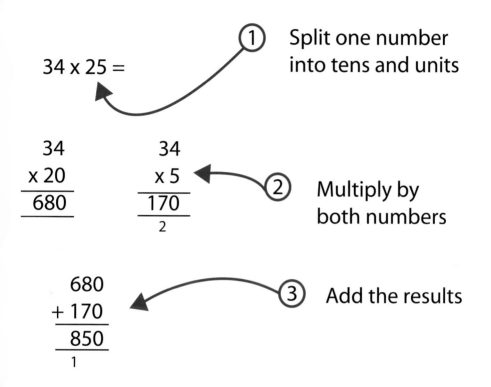

① Split one number into tens and units

34
x 20
680

34
x 5
170
2

② Multiply by both numbers

680
+ 170
850
1

③ Add the results

34 x 25 = 850

Long Multiplication (Grid Method)

34 x 25

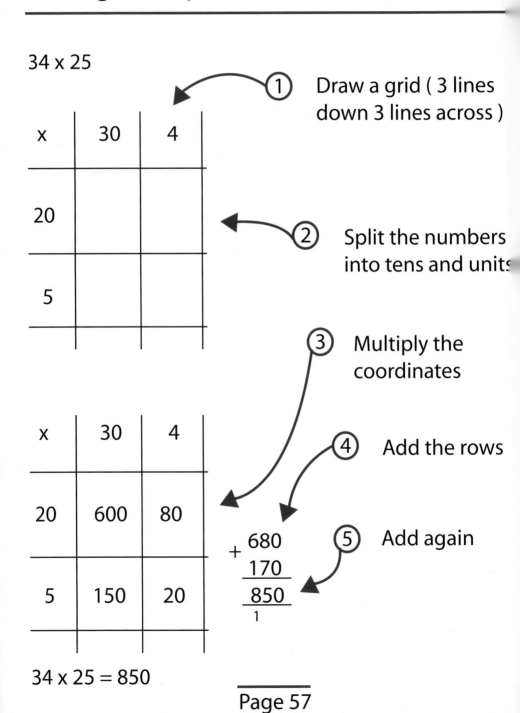

① Draw a grid (3 lines down 3 lines across)

② Split the numbers into tens and units

③ Multiply the coordinates

④ Add the rows

⑤ Add again

$$+ \begin{array}{r} 680 \\ 170 \\ \hline 850 \\ {\scriptstyle 1} \end{array}$$

x	30	4
20	600	80
5	150	20

34 x 25 = 850

Easy Rules for Dividing

÷ 2
If a number ends in
2, 4, 6, 8, 0

÷ 3
If you add the digits of a number and the answer is a
multiple of 3
e.g. $= 579 = 5 + 7 + 9 = 21$

÷ 5
If a number ends in 0 or 5

÷ 6
If you add the digits of an even number and answer is
a multiple of 3
e.g. $= 3492 = 3 + 4 + 9 + 2 = 18$

÷ 9
If you add the digits of a number and the answer is a
multiple of 9
e.g. $= 8856 = 8 + 8 + 5 + 6 = 27$

÷ 10
If a number ends in 0

Short Division

$462 \div 2$

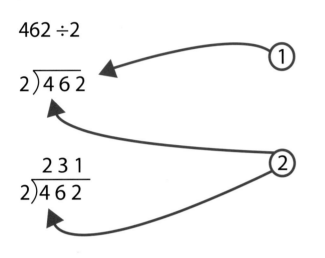

① Set it out

② ÷ each number separately starting with the nearest number

Remainders

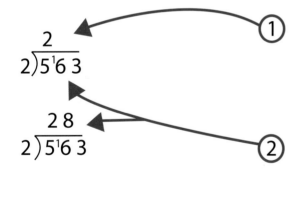

① Any remainder is written beside the next number

② In this case 16 is then divided by 2

③ If you are left with a remainder, write it at the end of the sum

Long Division

714 ÷ 17 = This method is sometimes called `bundles´ or `chunking´

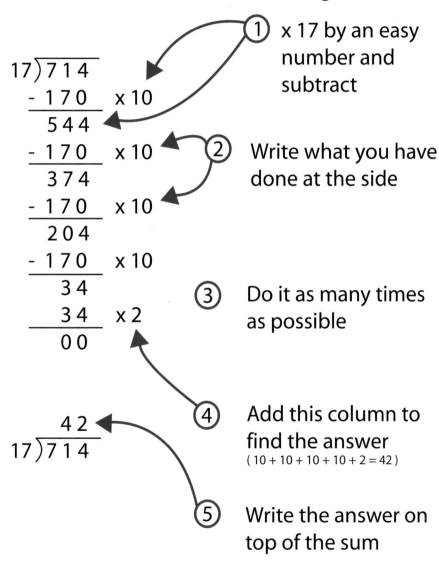

17)714
 - 170   x 10
   544
 - 170   x 10
   374
 - 170   x 10
   204
 - 170   x 10
    34
    34   x 2
    00

    42
17)714

① x 17 by an easy number and subtract

② Write what you have done at the side

③ Do it as many times as possible

④ Add this column to find the answer
(10 + 10 + 10 + 10 + 2 = 42)

⑤ Write the answer on top of the sum

Decimals   Addition

$6 \cdot 8 + 2 \cdot 93 + 11 \cdot 5$

```
      6·8
  +   2·93
     11·5
  ─────────
     21·23
     1 2
```

① Write out with the decimal points underneath each other

② +

$24 \cdot 2 + 3 + 5 \cdot 6$

```
     24·2
      3·0
  +
      5·6
  ─────────
     32·8
     1
```

① Remember that 3 i a whole number

② Set out as before

③ +

Decimals   Subtraction

18·7 – 4·2

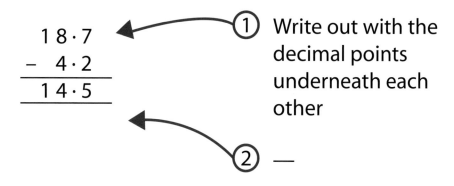

18·7
– 4·2

14·5

① Write out with the decimal points underneath each other

② —

6 – 1·3

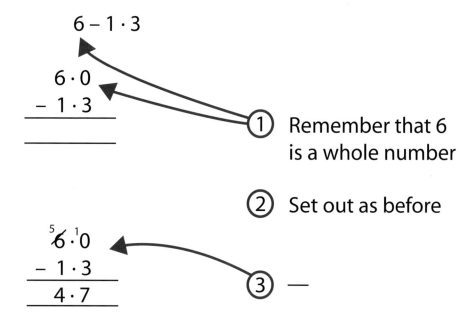

6·0
– 1·3
----

① Remember that 6 is a whole number

② Set out as before

⁵6·¹0
– 1·3

4·7

③ —

Decimals   Multiplication

Multiplying by 10 , 100 and 1000

x 10 = move the decimal point one place
to the right
$3 \cdot 26 \times 10 = 32 \cdot 6$

x 100 = move the decimal point two places
to the right
$4 \cdot 287 \times 100 = 428 \cdot 7$

x 1000 = move the decimal point three places
to the right
$6 \cdot 9473 \times 1000 = 6947 \cdot 3$

Fill in any empty spaces up to the
decimal point with noughts
$= 4 \cdot 5 \times 100 = 450$

Decimals   Multiplication

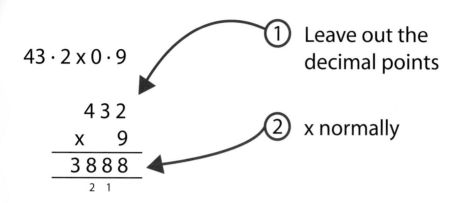

$43 \cdot 2 \times 0 \cdot 9$

① Leave out the decimal points

```
  4 3 2
x     9
-------
3 8 8 8
  2 1
```

② x normally

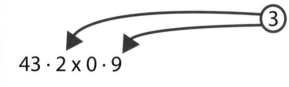

$43 \cdot 2 \times 0 \cdot 9$

③ Count the number of decimal places in the original sum

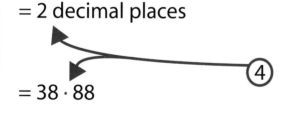

= 2 decimal places

= $38 \cdot 88$

④ Put the decimal point into the answer so it has the same number of decimal places

Decimals   Division

Dividing by 10 , 100 and 1000

$\div 10$ = move the decimal point one place to the left
$$64 \cdot 3 \div 10 = 6 \cdot 43$$

$\div 100$ = move the decimal point two places to the left
$$814 \cdot 2 \div 100 = 8 \cdot 142$$

$\div 1000$ = move the decimal point three places to the left
$$9658 \cdot 1 \div 1000 = 9 \cdot 6581$$

Fill in any empty spaces up to the decimal point with noughts
$$= 34 \cdot 2 \div 100 = 0 \cdot 342$$

Decimals   Division

Division by a whole number

$4 \cdot 5 \div 5$

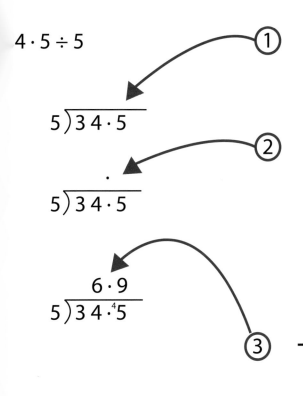

① Set it out normally

② Make sure that the decimal point in the answer is above the decimal point in the question

③ $\div$

$34 \cdot 5 \div 5 = 6 \cdot 9$

Decimals   Division

Division by a decimal number

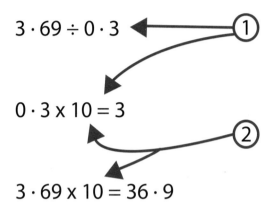

$3 \cdot 69 \div 0 \cdot 3$

① Make the right - han number into a whol number

$0 \cdot 3 \times 10 = 3$

② x the left - hand number by the same amount

$3 \cdot 69 \times 10 = 36 \cdot 9$

$3 \overline{)36 \cdot 9}$

③ Set it out normally

$3 \overline{)36 \cdot 9}^{\;\cdot}$

④ Make sure that the decimal point in the answer is above the decimal point in the question

$3 \overline{)36 \cdot 9}^{\,12 \cdot 3}$

⑤ ÷

$3 \cdot 69 \div 0 \cdot 3 = 12 \cdot 3$

Decimals to Fractions

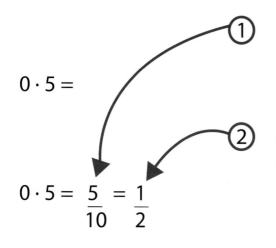

1. Write the decimal as a fraction

2. Cancel to lowest terms

$$0 \cdot 5 =$$

$$0 \cdot 5 = \frac{5}{10} = \frac{1}{2}$$

$$0 \cdot 0\,9 = \frac{9}{100}$$

$$0 \cdot 2\,5 = \frac{25}{100} = \frac{1}{4}$$

Fractions to Decimals

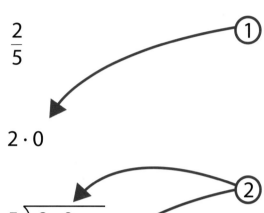

$\frac{2}{5}$

$2 \cdot 0$

① Make the top numb
look like a decimal
by putting · 0 after i

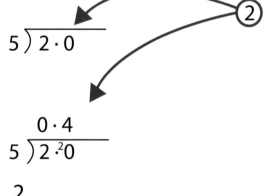

$5 \overline{)\, 2 \cdot 0}$

② ÷ that number by
the bottom number

$\begin{array}{r} 0 \cdot 4 \\ 5\overline{)\,2\,^{2}0} \end{array}$

$\frac{2}{5} = 0 \cdot 4$

Or

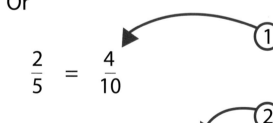

$\frac{2}{5} = \frac{4}{10}$

① Make the fraction in
an equivalent fractic

② Write as a decimal

$\frac{4}{10} = 4 \div 10 = 0 \cdot 4$

$\frac{2}{5} = 0 \cdot 4$

Scale

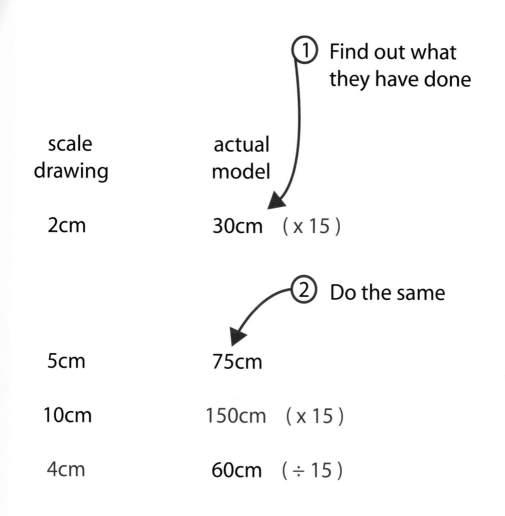

① Find out what they have done

scale drawing	actual model	
2cm	30cm	(x 15)

② Do the same

5cm	75cm	
10cm	150cm	(x 15)
4cm	60cm	(÷ 15)

Time   Distance   Speed

Time = distance ÷ speed
(Total distance travelled ÷ average speed)

Distance = speed x time
(Average speed x time of journey)

Speed = distance ÷ time
(Total distance travelled ÷ total time taken)

Here is an easy way to remember

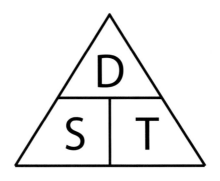

Distance = S x T
Speed = D over T
Time = D over S

Time

60 seconds = 1 minute

60 minutes = 1 hour

24 hours = 1 day

7 days = 1 week

4 weeks = 1 month

365 days = 1 year , 366 days = leap year

52 weeks = 1 year

12 months = 1 year

10 years = 1 decade

100 years = 1 century

1000 years = 1 millennium

Sum of

Addition

Plus

Add

$+$

Altogether

And

Total

More than

Increase

Subtraction

Fewer than

Take from

Take away

Deduct

$-$

Less than

Minus

Difference

Decrease

Reduce

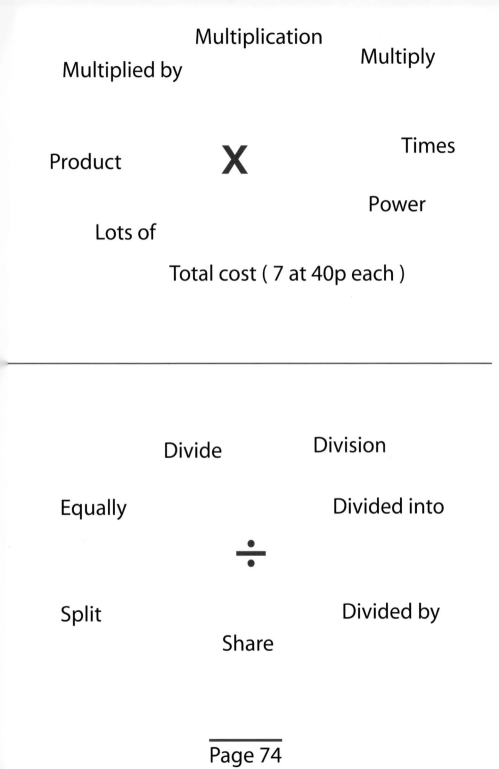

Multiplication

Multiplied by

Multiply

Product

X

Times

Power

Lots of

Total cost (7 at 40p each)

Divide

Division

Equally

Divided into

÷

Split

Divided by

Share

Helpful Rules

4 Rules of Maths

$$+ \quad - \quad X \quad \div$$

If there is no sign = **X**

short x and ÷ use tables up to 12

long x and ÷ use tables over 12

Problem Solving

Use + or x to make the answer bigger

Use – or ÷ to make the answer smaller

Metric Tables

Length

10 millimetres (mm) = 1 centimetre (cm)

100 centimetres (cm) = 1 metre (m)

1000 metres (m) = 1 kilometre (km)

Weight

1000 grams (g) = 1 kilogram (kg)

1000 kilograms (kg) = 1 tonne (t)

Capacity

10 millilitres (ml) = 1 centilitre (cl)

1000 millilitres (ml) = 1 litre (l)

Golden rules

Time

12hr clock = am/pm

24hr clock = 4 numbers
first two = hour ⟶ (21 : 43)
last two = minutes

Decimals

Always set them out with the decimal point in the same column

Brackets

Do them first

Months of the year

30 days have September,
April, June and November.

All the rest have 31
Except February alone
Which has 28 days clear
29 in each leap year.

You can also do this on your knuckles

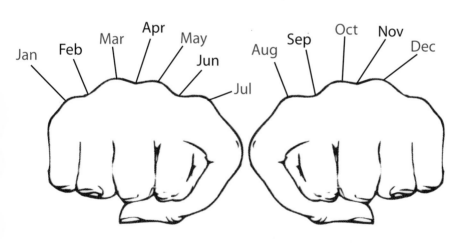

Jan Feb Mar Apr May Jun Jul Aug Sep Oct Nov Dec

All your knuckle bones = 31
Gap in between = 30 except for February
which has 28 days, or 29 in a leap year.

Here they are!

Also -
Many thanks to H and Dj for their endless encouragement and all those who helped with proof reading.

If you found this book useful and would like a few more copies for friends and relatives e-mail:- mrsjrules@hotmail.co.uk or go to www.mrsj.edenkent.org